Stocking Stuffers

Holiday Memoirs & Musings

A.J. Schmitz

MAXIXAM
PRESS

Dedicated to those who struggle mentally
and financially during the holidays.

Other books by A.J. Schmitz:

Buggin' Out

The Death of Our Dreams and Other Funny Stories

Nut Job

The Stupid Machine

Dear Norman

Everything in this book is true.

Some of the names have
been checked and
changed twice.

Contents

The Golden Banana
& Other Traditions

There's a classic photo of my mother holding up our Christmas tree that's just fallen over. It was 1980 and she managed to leap and catch it before it hit the ground, but not before the momentum pitched half the ornaments onto the floor. Seconds after we completed the task of decorating the crooked shrub, we stood back to admire it and *whooom* – down it went. My mother is yelling at the viewer (my father) who, instead of helping her with the tree, took the opportunity to grab the camera. My mother's eyes are wild with fire under a mop of blonde-permed hair that seemed to permeate the heads of everyone in the late 70s and early 80s. After that incident, we started a new tradition – lashing the tree to the wall with a wire. Most families have warm Christmas traditions like stuffing a goose, playing charades, or dressing up as Santa and Mrs. Claus and swinging with the neighbors. Good, wholesome fun. Ours was making sure the tree never fell again.

Another long-standing tradition we have in my family is keeping the bows from opened gifts. It's gotten to the point where we have enough bows to adorn a gift for every person in New York state. We buy new bows every year, yet we never discard old bows from previous years.

"Oh, this bow is gorgeous!" someone will squeal, tear it off the paper and squirrel it to the side.

After we finish unwrapping all the gifts, there's a pile of gifts and a pile of bows. The bow pile is added to the bows that have already been hoarded for the past 30 years. There's literally thousands of bows, all of them without their original sticky tape because they've either been torn off, or have old wrapping paper stuck to their bottoms. We have a giant bag of bows that goes so deep, each layer is a time capsule – the crusts and mantles of days long past. They're adorned with patterns, sheens, glitter and icons... style statements from the eras in which they came.

"Oh this is so 80s!" someone will say holding up a purple bow straight from Prince's neckerchief collection.

When wrapping gifts, my wife or mother will grab a bow from my hand and wistfully recall the gift it was originally paired with.

"I got this bow from the planter your mom gave me that rotted in the rain."

Along with bows, there's a stunning collection of ribbons, none of which can be used because either the person or the gift doesn't warrant the prestige.

"You're wrapping a baseball mitt with the golden antelope ribbon? That's for a nicer gift!"

"What gift should we save it for?" I ask.

"Something special."

"Like… a refrigerator? Or a bar of plutonium?"

Years of neglect and pressure weight from the top bows have reduced lower-level bows to crooked flowers. I'll yank a 1994 bow from the grab-bag and stick it on a freshly wrapped gift, but it seems off. It's perfect in every way, but one of the curled ribbons was stored incorrectly and is jutting at a weird angle from the rest of its symmetrical friends.

"That bow looks off," Rita will say.

That's code for *replace it immediately* which is unfortunate, because the bow has been in storage since Mariah Carey's first marriage – back when all she wanted was him. Now it's ready for the bow graveyard with all the other crooked bows; as well as the ribbons that are too short to circumference the average shirt box and random nametags bent at the corners like neglected books on a shelf.

I believe that tree-falling incident was one of the nails that constructed the coffin for the death of Christmas in my mother's heart. My mother wasn't, nor isn't a Grinch, and far from a Scrooge, but she's similar to many people around the holidays… already exhausted and forced to do an ungodly amount of work to decorate, keep up appearances, host events, eat and drink in abundance while battling crowds at the mall to procure gifts no appreciates. Just the thought of it is depressing, and in some ways, I don't blame her. Christmastime can be a real slog.

For years my parents hosted Christmas Eve dinner where half the Schmitz clan came to laugh, drink and air grievances across the table. Resentments ranged from: lack of screen time in old 8mm movies; the value of gifts received; and of course, like many households, how much love was *actually* given throughout the years. All of it while eating our traditional lasagna. We're not Italian, but lasagna seemed the way to go. Most Italians have the feast of the seven fishes, yet we ate one giant lasagna in a massive casserole tray, blackened on the edges from molten, gristle cheese. I believe it was the one dish that produced the least amount of complaints from everyone. Plus, it was cheap… 20 pounds of pasta, sauce and cheese and all 15 of the invited Schmitz brood was fed.

Over the years, the Christmas coffin nails came in small, incremental whacks. Because my father knew half the folks in town, and our combined families the size of a devoted cult, my mother was forced to write and address a few hundred Christmas cards until her hand curled into a trembling claw. The cards we received in return would paper the walls of our house like a crime investigation evidence board… connected with bright red ribbon and bows. When we received a card from someone who didn't get one from us, my mother would dash one off to the post office like a hot potato. It was a social/postal nightmare. I think it drove my mother insane.

When my mother was a kid, she'd awaken on Christmas morning with her four siblings, only to get dressed and filter past the Christmas tree with her eyes

4

closed so her parents could march them all to church, a horrifying act I can only characterize as torture. I'm not sure why my grandparents didn't execute a more reasonable Christmas morning ritual for their children – like pressing bamboo shoots under their fingernails. If you've never been to a Roman Catholic church for Christmas mass, it's similar to a virgin sacrifice, except not as visually stimulating and sans sacrificial virgin. There's chanting and moaning and grim men in long robes. Occasionally a Christmas carol rings through the air. This may have been the very first nail in the coffin in the death of Christmas in my mother's eyes, but it was most definitely the *final* nail in the coffin in her church-going ways. Once she became an adult, her only desire to enter a church was for a wedding or a funeral.

Only after my agitated mother and her squirmy siblings returned home from church could they open their Christmas gifts – still dressed in stiff Sunday-best clothing while other kids lounged in their pajamas and filth, like pigs in their own shit.

On the other side of town, my father and his siblings were tearing the living room to pieces like wild hogs at a feeding. The afore-mentioned pigs in shit. When my Uncle Ed was 4, he asked his older brothers: "What should I get dad for Christmas?" My father and his brothers, being the helpful and kind older siblings they were, told Ed: "Dad really enjoys buttered toast." Sure enough, minutes after the Christmas tree went up, there was a small square packet under the tree '*from: Edward; to Dad.*' Needless to say, when it was opening 40 days later, it was a petrified knot of mold. My grandfather appreciated the gesture none-the-less.

My paternal grandmother Kathy "Tix" Schmitz was a certifiable Christmas junkie. She had literal truckloads of catalogs delivered to her house via the United States Postal Service. Tix kept most of the United States mail order companies in business on her own. Thank the Lord she never figured out how to use the internet. Amazon would have built a warehouse in her backyard to simplify the process.

For Tix, the Christmas shopping started at the beginning of the year. Actually, the mili-second the current Christmas ended. She'd get on the phone with the next available representative, bark out SKU numbers, and before you could un-deck the halls, boxes were coming to the door like they were on a perpetual conveyor belt. She didn't just know the mailman by name, she knew the entire department and could identify their charred remains through dental records. The packages were ceaseless, all through the year. They came in boxes, packages and bags. But they didn't always come with tags. As the piles overtook her home, she'd forget whom some of the gifts were for. One year my cousin Billy got three identical track suits. Some would consider that a decent haul, but I think all Billy wanted that year was a guitar.

Tix would also watch the completely irrational Home Shopping Network, whose vampire-like hosts prompted viewers to phone-in nervous purchases believing the limited supply of (insert garbage here) would run out. Any one of her six children, in-laws and 14 grandchildren were either blessed or cursed by these impulse buys. Neon sweaters, Ginsu knives, dangling earrings or some sort of barking toy dog could be in anyone's lap regardless of sex or age.

About two weeks before Christmas, Tix would enact the traditional gift-wrapping call-to-arms. All the women of the family would come and help her wrap the gifts she acquired over 12 months. It was a combination of coffee klatch, assembly line, and detective case as the girls opened boxes, identified objects, assigned them to a giftee, then wrapped and bowed them all. It took many days, multiple pots of coffee, the occasional cocktail and eventually overtime.

It drove my mother crazy how many gifts we all got. Our house was overrun with stuff. It was one of those coffin nails that drove her towards the edge. My mother enjoyed uncluttered environments, clean spaces and minimalistic touches. We had stuff on top of stuff. And when the space ran out, we'd stuff that stuff into boxes to make room for more stuff. On top of that, Tix always managed to find a few gifts randomly stashed somewhere. Like a magician, she'd pull it out three days after Christmas and say "oh, I forgot I had this under my bed." Nine times out of ten, it was for my sister Caroline, which drove me crazy even though I had already received 30 gifts.

Unfortunately, my mother's father was also a

self-professed "QVC" shopper. We'd enter Grandpa's house to find him upside down, having purchased gravity boots and locked into a giant flippable inversion rack that took up the entire living room. During Christmas, he'd buy 50 of one item and give everyone the same gift. One year it was pocketknives... the next, crosses on chains. He'd scan the stock market scroll on some soulless TV news channel and any infomercial touting the benefits of wonky exercise equipment or the precious value of collectable coins was soon in the mail and in the hands of his family.

But one of the big... and I mean *railroad spike* nails in the proverbial coffin of my mother's Christmas death was the golden banana.

The golden banana was a garish, gold plastic tree ornament that managed to survive the 1940s and linger into the 1980s. For some reason, we hung on our tree. It was the type of thing Bing Crosby had in bowl with other metallic fruit next to his sparkling white Christmas tree bubbling with neon-red bulbs. The golden banana was an example of mid-century modern design – the kind of visions-of-the-future depicted in art diagrams of self-driving cars where the family played checkers at the center table of their glass-domed vehicle and homes had conversation pits around a hi-fi stereo while served aspic by robot servants.

My mother professed her hatred of the golden banana so many times, it became a rite of passage to hang it directly in the middle of the tree – front and center. A Christmas tradition of mockery. Whenever it was uncovered from the ornament box, one of us would hold it high like the Holy Grail and shout "the golden banana!" My mother would turn spruce blue and shout "not the banana!" her eyes glaring LED bulbs of hate, similar to the photo of the tree falling incident.

The golden banana was both stupid and wonderful... a design engineers dream and a stylist's nightmare.

A banana-sized banana, it was an obnoxious, gleaming gold turd whose stem curled into its own built-in hook. It didn't need a flimsy wire hook or any type of accessory. Once removed from the ornament box, it was hung in mere seconds... well before my mother had a chance to stop its placement. Morally, once it was on the tree, it couldn't be removed. My mother knew we loved the banana because of its ridiculousness. If she never said a word about her hatred of the banana, it would have disappeared shortly after *The Year Without A Santa Clause* hit the airwaves. Because it raised her ire to Heat-Miser levels of anger, it was forever part of our Christmas decorating tradition.

One year I came home from school to find the golden banana in the garbage, a sliver of gold peeking under some rubbish. When I discovered it, my mother screamed "it's broken!" and I uncovered a perfectly in-tact banana with nary a scratch on it. It went right back on the tree. I'm not sure why my mother hated it so much. Perhaps she had taste. Even a mention of the golden banana would darken her mood for days. It was perplexing. I don't think she hated bananas... we ate them constantly. I don't think she was

assaulted by the banana or anything resembling a golden banana. From what I remember, she enjoyed gold jewelry and
the James Bond film *The Man With The Golden Gun*. It was
a mystery to all of us. I think she just thought it was ugly and
dumb and didn't want to back down from her stance.

Regardless, the golden banana eventually disappeared without a trace. There was no explaining its ab-
sence. One Christmas season it was there, the next season
it was gone. When we inquired about the golden banana's
whereabouts, my mother shrugged innocently with her
palms raised towards Jesus and said "I don't know" … a
performance so transparent, if she were on trial for murder,
the blood on her hands would have dripped to the floor in
streams.

Decades later, I tried to introduce another golden
banana ornament to the family, but it wasn't the same. It
didn't have the old banana's sleek design atheistic, sexy
sheen, or futuristic ingenuity. The original was a masterwork
they created back in the day before people truly understood
taste… back when stuff never broke, except for the mold in
which the precious golden banana was made. The golden
banana was forged in times when a thermos could survive a
nuclear blast and grandma's bullet-proof olive-green refrigerator was handed down from generation to generation.

Today, we have so many Christmas tree ornaments,
we don't know what to do with half of them. We're on five
generations of hand-me-down ornaments at this point in
time. They range from tasteful to gaudy; from dime-store

garbage to museum pieces. They're forged metal, hand-blown glass, crystal and wood. There's historical cartoon characters and various Santas doing something in range of 40 activities, including: surfing, baking, and hot air ballooning. As the decorations have trickled down, my wife and I have procured the least desired tree ornaments of others but have such an abundance we now have *two* Christmas trees. The golden banana is hardly missed these days.

Growing up, my father went to work at 8:00 in the morning and didn't return until 6:00 in the evening. That left my mother to do a lot of the Christmas decorating. Unfortunately, she had a job as well. She found Christmas decorating to be rather thankless task. Now that they're both pushing 80, they've eased their decorating burden considerably. They got rid of the towering 11-foot Christmas tree and purchased a much more reasonable 10-foot tree. The 11-foot tree was an unruly 500 pound beast with five skin-gouging sections, whereas the 10-footer *also* has five skin-gouging sections, but it's a svelte 475 pounds. When my father came home with the 10-footer, my mother threatened divorce. I wasn't there when he dragged it into the house, but I'm sure her face looked similar to the picture I referenced earlier. The 10-foot tree still requires a ladder to decorate most of the tree, something my mother didn't want her husband to do considering he's blown-out his Achilles tendon, has undergone hernia surgery requiring 20 stitches, has the eyesight of Stevie Wonder and the reflexes of a panda bear on hard tranquilizers. The new tree she envisioned was something in the 5-foot range. Maybe a dwarf pine in a pot. If she had her wish, a picture of a fully decorated tree tacked to the wall would've sufficed.

Like my wife, my father is a self-proclaimed "lover of Christmas." He refuses to cut back on the back-breaking ornamental decorating and neither will she. He'll end up in the hospital and the doctor will ask if he hurt himself on the icy sidewalk and he'll confess it was from hanging a giant snowflake above the door. My wife has more Santas than your average department store. She has Santas in hiking gear, Santa reading to a small child, and Santa consuming coffee and drinking wine. Like the pinecone that didn't fall far from the pine tree, I take after my mother. Sure, I love Christmas, but I don't want to spend it in the hospital due to a nervous breakdown… although if my father is there recovering from a fall, we could room together. Between the credit card bills, the running around, school pageants, and the so called 'traditions' it's enough to drain every drop of energy from your already drained body.

Our friends the Lawrences' would do a traditional Christmas morning polar bear plunge. They'd wrangle their lunatics friends and dive off a pier into frigid Huntington Bay. On the only year I participated (and I know this is going to sound like hyperbole) I believe I temporarily died. This was in my lean years, nary a scrap of meat on my bones. I've never been a person with a lot of "extra cushioning" around me, so the ice-cold water locked my body into some form of icicle coma. Stumbling back onto the beach, I couldn't feel anything from the neck down, yet ironically, I was also in agonizing pain. I was fully aware that I was walking on my legs, but they were totally numb. I let my brain to do what it does instinctually, swinging the legs forward and that type of thing, until I arrived to the back of a station wagon where a full bar of syrupy liquors awaited the morons who dove into the ice bath. I chugged Schnapps and Cognac until I regained the feeling in my legs, which felt similar to someone hammering my knees caps like a xylophone. Once I defrosted, I realized I was drunk and spent the rest of the day on the couch straightening out my pre-noon drunkenness.

Eventually the polar bear plunge stopped as did the hand-written card exchanges and the lasagna dinners. Some of that is due to age. The people involved are old or they're gone. Jumping into frozen water isn't good for 75 year-olds. But, it's also a case of the 35 year-olds implementing the tradition of staying on the couch in their pajamas all day and refusing to go outside.

Some traditions die hard and some fade away. New people start new traditions. I believe some of these new traditions have lightened the load not only for my mother, but for all the people who felt compelled to kill themselves at Christmas and other big holidays. Instead of marching to church on Christmas morning, the kids ask, "can we stay in our pajamas for the next 3 day?" and the parents say "yes" because they *too* would like to stay in their pajamas for the next 3 days.

Instead of writing endless personalized cards and mailing them, we shout a hearty *Merry Christmas* to everyone on Facebook and call it a job well done. That's a tradition I can get behind and so can my mother. If you didn't see the Facebook message, or didn't hear from us directly, let it be known that we *implied* that we wish everyone a Merry Christmas... through osmosis. Don't be offended.

Ironically, I'll go to my sister's house and see a card on the wall from someone we both know (a multi-frame picture setup of the kids and the dog, all of whom have grown a foot and a half since last year) and I'll get offended and ask: "why didn't I get a card?"

The answer, of course, is because I didn't send one to *them*. What goes around comes around. A Christmas tradition that also involves Karma.

The Magic
of Christmas

They say it's better to give than to receive, and that goes double at Christmas time. That's the magic of Christmas – the giving. I'm at the age where I don't want anything. I'm happy to not only give gifts, but take the things I own and give them to other people – right off my walls.

"This is a cool poster."

"Take it, it's yours."

"Really?"

"Yeah, Merry Christmas."

"But it's July."

My Uncle Paul is the same way. He has a small forest of guitars and gives them to people like pediatrician lollipops. If you're not careful, you can walk into his apartment for a cup of tea and leave with some kind of Rickenbacker that John Lennon strummed in 1964. It's the gift of music.

But this type of thing happens to most people as they get older. Not the guitar-giving thing, but the not-needing-gifts thing. You reach a point where you can't possibly squeeze another item into your life. Except maybe a new liver, but those are terribly expensive and I don't expect one to be handed to me in a glittery box with bows.

Any gift I receive now is taken with a warped sense of anger because it forces me to fake a smile and find a place to jam it in my heaping piles of crap. Someone gifts me wine or a rugged pair of socks with reinforced toes and I smile like a beauty pageant winner. These intelligent gift-givers warm the cockles of my heart. They have good taste and good sense. If anyone hands me a trinket, it will most likely be at my future garage sale that I plan to have in about a decade. I should probably plan that sale now, because it will be epic. I'll empty my attic and it will be the sale of the century. I'll need to borrow every rummage sale card table in town to fit all the stuff I own. I'll sell everything and make $50 and wonder why I spent 10 days prepping for a garage sale that netted me about 30 cents for every hour of sweat I poured into it.

My father is impossible to shop for. I usually default to historical books about war, which he then recites verbatim at Christmas dinner the following year.

"You know that World War I basically started by accident?"

"Really?"

"Yeah, because…"

And then we pass the wine around the table and fill our goblets to the brim.

Any gift given to me that I can't eat or drink is a

waste. Even as a kid I wanted those sausage and cheese gift sets that come on a bed of shredded paper in cheery red boxes. I was a weird kid. Instead of meat, I got Legos, which was great, but to pair the Legos with a smoky cheddar and dried salami would have made my Christmas wishes come true.

Now, *I'm* the guy who's impossible to shop for. My wife's Christmas list is essentially the home page of Bloomingdale's website, and my Christmas list says GLOVES in faint pencil on a sticky note. She goes to the mall and gets me a fabulous button-down shirt that I hang honorably next to my Boston College sweatshirt that my niece gave me five years ago that I wear every day. My closet has amazing taste but I'm personally a missed beard trim from resembling a homeless person.

I live vicariously through gift giving now. I get people what I wanted when I was 17.

"Oh look, the *Die Hard* film box set."

"You're welcome Aunt Ginny."

My son is rounding into a proper nerd at the age of 13. I got him a vintage Godzilla poster for Christmas and his head nearly exploded. Paired with the collectible Godzilla figure, mint in the box with Japanese writing, his other gifts could have been donated to the Salvation Army.

I gift my friends random memoirs about drug addict musicians and tragic movie stars and they nod confused. They don't realize that I plan to borrow the book, and when their memory gets hazy from all the heavy booze and holi-day foods, they'll forget I ever borrowed the book. It's a gift for everyone.

I often go Christmas shopping for myself, wrap the item and slide it under the tree. My family scratch their heads and wonder why there's a new gift 'To: A.J., From: Luke Skywalker.' On Christmas morning, everyone gathers around when I tear open my mystery package and reveal a coffee table book on the history of robots in pop culture.

"Wow!" I exclaim, "Just what I wanted... thanks, Luke!"

Even though I don't have much money, I try and give a little when I can. I jam some cash in a card and hand it to the girls at my local deli. It's a nice way of saying "Thanks for the 85 egg sandwiches you made me over the year. I appreciate the fact you smell like bacon every day of your life." Some men find that scent a turn-on. How could they not? But the women at the deli prefer to smell like women and not roasted pig 365 days out of the year. Hopefully they put the money towards perfume.

Working in the many offices of Manhattan over the years, I was always part of a Secret Santa gift exchange. This can be hit or miss in so many glorious ways. Whenever someone got *me* as the receiver, they jammed a few bottles of dense German beer into a gift bag on their walk to the office the morning of the exchange. That's smart shopping right there. I would always get someone as my Secret Santa that I disliked in the office... someone I deemed either lazy or inadvertently making my job more difficult by being a clueless moron. I'd be forced to slink around the office and question my workmates to gain insight into this person's hobbies and twisted fetishes.

"You think Agnes likes porn? What about *Die Hard* movies?"

One year I got my Secret Santa – as well as everyone I knew and loved – beef jerky for Christmas. My buddy Ned and I were on a major beef jerky kick, ordering premium beef jerky from a website in Tennessee where you could fill your cart with jerky from around the country. Just about every animal within rifle range was dried into salty, leathery strips for our protein pleasure. Besides the obvious beef, we chewed smoky alligator, snapped into gamey Elk, noshed on spicy wild boar, and even delved into fish and fish skins.

When Eve, my Secret Santa at HBO opened her box of jerky, it unfolded like a movie scene of someone beiing shot in slow motion. It took a solid 30 seconds for her to comprehend what she was being gifted. After she parted the red tissue paper and filtered through the brown slab packets and vacuumed sealed sticks donning images of pigs and deer, her face knotted into what I can only describe as... a proper British lady on Safari being handed an elephant heart to bite into after a kill... and accepting it so as not to offend the locals. She thanked me and burst into laughter so as not to cry. Perhaps the red tissue paper was a poor choice as it gave the illusion of digging into a bloody animal sternum to reveal the meaty insides. In hindsight I find it brilliant. This was the reaction of most recipients upon getting my delicious meat packages that Christmas. My father was rendered speechless, which is a hard thing to do, and my grandmother insisted I'd lost my mind, which was true because I'd been eating nothing but salty jerky for months on end.

The embers of my glowing heart were cooled by these reactions. Not *one* person could appreciate the beauty of Kangaroo sticks in Korean soy sauce, Spicy Pepper Ostrich, or even the more palatable Smoked Duck. Sure, their blood pressure may have risen 10 or 15 points, but that's a small price to pay for delicacies of that nature.

Perhaps these were gifts I actually wanted for myself. Like those snuggly-packed Hickory Farms meat boxes I longed for as a kid. But, that's the beauty of being an adult. Once you reach a certain age you can buy this crap for yourself. You'll also be an adult and realize you can't eat a box of dried meat because you'll end up like a hibernating bear on the couch for two days as your body breaks down the meat…. or worse, on the toilet while your body rejects it.

•••

You would think that a fat man who lives at the North Pole and circles the globe in a sled pulled by flying reindeer would be enough magic to dazzle the mind, but apparently not. For some reason, we need to continually add to this magic by introducing more magic. It started in 1939 when the cuddly and endearing mega-corporation Montgomery Ward Department Store asked copywriter Robert May to come up with a promotional gimmick, which birthed unto the world the annoying character *Rudolph the Red-Nosed Reindeer*. They sang songs about Rudolph and praised his glowing red proboscis, which guided Santa around and through earth's difficult weather patterns. I'm sure Rudolph's nose and Amsterdam's red-light district created all sorts of logistical issues that waylaid Santa for hours, killing precious time when he should've been bombing gifts down chimneys under tight time constraints.

Once the Animated Rankin/Bass holiday special hit the airwaves in 1964, it took a quaint, secondary animal character into the stratosphere of popularity. I admit, *Rudolph the Red Nosed Reindeer* is a charming little Christmas special that has enough cuteness to power a 747 airbus around the planet... even if you can see every little dirty fingerprint on the felt puppet faces on our giant, modern HD Televisions. Yukon Cornelius alone has enough charm to carry an off-shoot special or two, and Hermey's pursuit of dental education probably increased dental school enrollment by leaps and bounds.

Every child looked up to see if a red dot might be seen in the darkened December night sky – filling their hearts with wonder. Before Rudolph, catching Santa doing his dirty work or zipping across the sky was a high priority, but suddenly, a reindeer with a red nose took the top spot in the UFO search. Rudolph snatched the thunder from a man who'd put some real time and effort into his notoriety. Working tirelessly 365 days a year, Santa slaved for hundreds of years to supply the world's children with toys – then, Wham! Forgotten like a caboose with square wheels. Every tabletop decoration, framed print, or yellowing postcard made before 1964 depicting Santa and his reindeer sans Rudolph, was met with confusion and disapproval by children far and wide.

"Where's Rudolph?" they'd cry. "How can Santa possibly fly without a proper lighting system to guide his sleigh?"

I admit, I was one of those little brats fascinated by Rudolph. After my 30th inquiry about why Rudolph was missing from some 1945 ornament or statuette, my father basically said:

"Listen, Rudolph is something that came out a few years ago. It's a story. We're not even sure if Rudolph is real. Before the story of Rudolph, it was just Santa and his eight reindeer. That's why all these things have the original Santa."

That was enough to not only shut me up, but snatch a tiny piece of Christmas magic away from my greedy little hands. After that, I looked at these Santa depictions differently. Pre- and Post-Rudolph years. Similar to Europe Pre- and Post-World War II.

Again, a fat guy in a red suit flying the skies in a

sled powered by magical flying reindeer, one with a glowing red nose, was not enough magic. Dash 40 years forward and we've added more magic to the holiday season with *Elf on a Shelf*. These spying elves move around at night and cause different levels of mischief. During the day, they watch over us and report any bad behavior to Santa with an itemized list of infractions. Previously it was only Santa that had the magic, but apparently elves have magic too… disregarding the fact that they're elves, a creature that doesn't actually exist in the world. These little elves fly around like Tinker Bell and sprinkle fairy dust and work in close relation with the FBI to monitor our every move.

Of course children think these elves are wonderfully charming. They awaken each day to see the elves involved in a new activity: feeding the cat, knocking bulbs off the tree, or performing strap-on anal sex with one other. We often forget to move the elves and my son wonders what happened; why didn't they move? We need to explain that they don't move *every* night… sometimes they're happy where they are. Sometimes they drink too much wine and are too zonked to get up and move their lazy asses.

Eventually *Elf on a Shelf* got an animated special too, filled with cuddly, charming elves and their mission to report all the good and bad to Santa… like a bunch of snitches. Of course, like any good marketing scheme, they introduced a girl, which is EXACTLY like the boy except she has lipstick and long eye lashes. The introduction of a reindeer was expected because we need more reindeer at Christmas.

Pretty soon they'll have dream kitchen homes in Malibu and children will grow up disappointed when their dreams of having a house on the beach in Malibu is replaced with a rotting shack in Dayton, Ohio. One thing these shelf-straddling elves don't have is feet. For some reason their legs taper down to nubs like land-mine victims. It's disturbing.

I'm not sure what magical thing they'll introduce next. There's only so much space in the magical Christmas manger. Speaking of the manger, this is supposed to be a holiday celebrating Jesus, a man born to a virgin, inseminated by God. That's pretty magical! The most magical part of the story being Joseph sticking around through all this stuff. He's a better man than I am – and my middle name is Joseph! He pulled a pregnant woman, carrying a baby that wasn't his, through the desert on a donkey, and slept with dirty animals on a pile of hay. I would have checked out of the situation a long time ago and checked into a motel. The nativity scene we own doesn't depict any doctors standing around, so I assume Joseph did the birthing as well. But I suppose that's the moral of the story. Joey's dedication to Jesus and Mary, and maybe knowing that three kings were going to show up with gold and other gifts – things he could use to get out of debt and maybe buy a small house somewhere.

I've heard Tel Aviv is very nice in December.

•••

Not only am I budget deficient to be a proper Santa, I'm also girth deficient. Regardless of how many creamy nogs, hearty stouts and gravy-covered potatoes I eat, it fails to make a bowl of jelly around my midsection. Not only that, I barely have time to do the things on my personal 'to-do' list, so being Santa with an unruly list of roughly one billion children to gift is way beyond my personal abilities.

Fortunately, we have the Santa's of the world to help us out. In America we have the big man in red who drops down your chimney. If you don't have a chimney, you must invent a way for him to get into your house when a child invariably asks: "What if you don't have a chimney?"

The excuses I've defaulted to range from "He uses magic" to "he has keys to every home!" In my more unprepared, nog-influenced moments, I've blurted out "he opens a window and climbs in" – like a drunk husband home from a late night bender. This appears to be strictly an American problem. Most cultures don't have the American version of Santa where his eight reindeer climb on your poorly engineered roof and access your house via chimney.

In Russia, a demon wizard named Ded Moroz comes to kidnap naughty children. What this has to do with the magic of Christmas, I have no idea, but he sounds more like an evil character from *The Lord of the Rings* and I believe you can summon him at other times by playing Led Zeppelin's *Stairway to Heaven* backwards on a record player. Either way, it's a warm-hearted tradition in the Slavic regions. Nowadays Ded travels with Snegurochka the Snow

Maiden, who gives gifts to the children, but is probably a witch that should be burned at the stake.

In Finland, the holiday tradition is Joulupukki, or Yule Goat – the Finnish Santa. Although not a demon wizard, Yule Goat was a vengeful spirit associated with the Norse god Odin who banged on doors and demanded gifts and food from Yuletide feasts. How this tradition started is unclear, but these days he is more of a giver than a receiver – a relief to paranoid young Finnish children. Like America's Santa, Yule Goat gets around by sleigh but his reindeer don't fly, which makes him an easy target. Modern day celebrations have Yule Goat depictions made of straw and lit on fire, very likely to burn any witches that might be in the immediate area.

In Sweden, Jultomten is a garden gnome known to do the Devil's dirty work and comes in a sleigh pulled by goats and protects farmhouses from bad luck. This tradition seems a little backwards as Satan is usually not a protector of bad things but a purveyor of bad things. But Satan and Santa have very similar spellings and both are red, so perhaps the two icons are not that far apart in nature. Today, Jultomten the gnome gives gifts to kids who are good throughout the year.

In Iceland, they seemed to have combined all of these nutty ideas into one. The 13 Yule Lads are a pack of mischievous elves who play tricks on children. Like Yule Goat, they'll steal your food or get Gryla, their mother to kidnap you if you behave badly. How kidnapping and ransom became joyous traditions in these places is hard to comprehend, but these are lands known to be -50 degrees Celsius in the summer, so the people and their brains are functioning in strange and mysterious ways.

Of course, who are we to judge other Santa cultures? The American Santa is a fat elf who flies on a sled pulled by reindeer. He smokes a pipe while stuffing stockings. That reminds me of a carpenter I used to work with who smoked all day on the job. He basically blinked non-stop because smoke was constantly in his eyes while he nailed things to a wall using a high-powered nail gun that could kill someone if used improperly.

A lot of countries have Santa wearing clothing more in line to be the next Pope. They have golden canes and towering bishop hats... things priests and witch doctors love. The American Santa is based on a monk named St. Nicholas from the year 80 AD, a time when everyone wore robes because fashion hadn't really been invented yet. St. Nick was the patron saint of children and helped the poor.

As the years wore on and storybooks and advertisements depicting Santa became more prominent, he eventually morphed into a chubby, red-suited man. Much of what we honor about Santa comes from Dutch culture. The name Santa Claus derives from the name Sinter Klaas, who I believe was also a character in the film *Die Hard*, the greatest Christmas movie ever made. Yes, Virginia, the best...

In Italy, instead of Santa, a good-natured witch named La Befana flies around on a broomstick and gifts toys to children. It's obvious the lazy Italians just carried over their Halloween traditions and shoehorned them into Christmas traditions. Speaking of shoehorning, our American Santa Claus gives naughty kids coal in their stocking while the 13 Icelandic Yule Lads jam rotten potatoes into the shoes of naughty children. In France, Père Noël appears in a red cloak and stuffs gifts in kids shoes, but travels with Père Fouettard, a nasty sidekick named "the whipping father" who beats children who've been bad all year. Call me crackers, but I prefer a nice lump of coal over a lump on the head.

In Austria, they like to mix their paganism as much as the next country by parading Krampus around. Krampus, a horned, anthropomorphic satanic goat appears on the same night as St. Nicolas, his supposed twin brother. Again, we have the Satan/Santa thing happening. While St. Nick is a delightful, jolly old elf who bestows gifts to children, Krampus has been known to dish out beatings to children who are bad. The Krampus warns: "do better next year" and if I was viciously beaten by a devilish goat near Christmas, I'd redouble my efforts to clean up my act. I know it's better to give than to receive, but I don't think that appraisal was made with beatings by Satanic sheep in mind. To celebrate the Krampus, people don frightening wooden masks and smear ashes on people who get too close. Obviously this sounds more like a human sacrifice ritual than a Christmas celebration. Toss a pentagram on the floor and this observance could open a portal to hell. For some reason the Austrians felt this was akin to stringing cranberries and popcorn across the fireplace. Austria is also the country where Hitler was born and raised, and there's no doubt he was beaten by Krampus in his formative years.

In my wife's home country of Brazil, they have Papai Noel, which is exactly like the American Santa except he comes in through the window (like the drunk husband) as Brazil is a tropical country that doesn't really have chimneys. In England, Santa goes by Father Christmas and is usually draped in green with a ring of ivy over his head – similar to the drunk husband, except he didn't make it through the window and instead slept in the bushes.

Like many countries, children give Santa their desired wish lists and hope they'll be fulfilled.

In Asia, Christmas is a mixed bag. In the Philippines, they straight up celebrate Santa Claus and he comes to bring good cheer. He doesn't always leave gifts, he just shows up waving and is as happy as a fat man can be. Fly the sleigh up a bit to China and Christmas is still a bit of a mystery. The younger Chinese generations celebrate a bit by hanging stockings for Dun Che Lao Ren, the "Christmas Old Man," but the elders find it a confusing ritual. In America, every Chinese restaurant from New York to Los Angeles is packed with Jews on Christmas Day, so perhaps the Chinese don't quite know what to make of Christmas yet. The children in China give apples wrapped in colorful cellophane as gifts, and anyone living in a country where people aren't dying of starvation, an apple is a boring gift, but for China, where anything from a bat to dirt could be on the dinner menu, it brings tremendous joy. Back in ancient England, fruit like oranges were a common gift and were sometimes used as an ornament for the Christmas tree. Considering half the population most likely died from scurvy, a healthy orange packed with vitamin C was considered not only an excellent gift, but medicine.

In Korea, Christmas is a fairly new holiday where Santa wears a blue costume. In Japan, Christmas Eve is a romantic holiday for Japanese couples to exchange gifts with each other. They have Santa Kurohsu or Hoteiosho, a Buddhist monk who watches children with eyes in the back of his skull, which conjures not sugar plums dancing, but incredibly creepy imagery in my head. Thailand is almost completely Buddhist, but since they're a country that likes to party, they celebrate Christmas anyway… my kinds of people. You may not catch a glimpse of Santa Claus in Thailand, but you may see dancing elephants – whether you've been drinking heavily or not. Rounding back towards the USA again, the Hawaiians call Santa Claus Kanakaloka. They say Mele Kalikimaka and have been known to decorate a palm tree or two.

The tradition of decorating trees can be traced back to the ancient Egyptians. Because evergreens remain green in the winter months, they were considered special and boughs were used to decorate homes. The early Romans who celebrated Saturnalia, or the Solstice, did the same. Even the murderous Vikings considered the evergreen tree a symbol of everlasting life and decorated accordingly. The 16th century Germans felt the same about these trees so naturally they chopped them down and dragged them into their homes. It's been said that Martin Luther had the brilliant idea to decorate the trees with candles. What better way to celebrate Christmas than stuffing a dry tree into your wooden home and lacing it with flaming sticks?

Eventually the Christmas tree found its way across Europe and into American homes by the early 1800s. Now Santa stuffs the gifts under the Christmas tree, which is more kindling to start a fire.

They say it's better to give than to receive and that's true. Between the generous tag team of Santa Claus and myself, my son gets about 30 presents. I look forward to the day we eliminate Santa from the equation. One, because it will save me money and; two, because the millisecond my son is done opening his presents, he picks up his phone and plays video games, neglecting everything that is strewn across the floor.

•••

The day after Christmas is the ultimate post-orgasm clarity. The month-long buildup to gifts and merriment ends with a rampage of paper-tearing and exhaustion. A joy explosion. You look around on December 26th and the twinkling lights have lost their luster. Nothing says holiday hangover like entering your living room bleary-eyed and nauseous on

January 1st and seeing a fully decorated tree in your living room.

"Who the hell is going to clean this thing up?" you think.

And the answer is YOU.

That's when the magic of Christmas is truly over.

There's nothing more depressing than pulling ornaments off a tree under the blanket of frigid gray winter skies.

When the decorations are going up, you're driven by an unknown force of cheer – fueled by goblets of wine and chocolate. Arctic temperatures when the tree is being trimmed are tolerable because it's all about joy… toss more marshmallows into the kettle of cocoa and splash another shot of whisky into a glass. There's no place like home for the holidays. There's a mystical energy to the proceedings. Fa la la la la and all that.

Declutter the house of Santas and reindeer on January 15th and you feel like an idiot. Christmas felt like two months ago and your house still looks like an elf mansion. You look around and all you see is labor-intensive work. You can still down a few goblets of wine, but the ring of the holiday is a distant thud, and you're not in the mood to trudge boxes up into attic storage.

My neighbors kicked their tree to the curb the day after Christmas and although that's a little premature, they've got the right idea. The calendar flipping to the new year is fertile ground for a fresh start. While fireworks burst and champagne pops on New Year's Eve, my house looks like it did the day after Thanksgiving when we immediately started decorating for Christmas – all while still jamming stuffing and turkey down our throats. It's hard to move on in life when an army of nutcrackers stare at you like a firing squad and your throw pillows say Happy Holidays.

The gingerbread house, which was so fresh and charming a month ago, is now a petrified forest. The icicles that hang from the eaves that we created using the piping bag are now lethal weapons – sharper than thorns and will sting us like hornets. The gumdrop hedges we built along the pathway to the door are still an excellent design choice, but it's offset by the candied holly wreath that someone glued to the front using an excessive amount of goopy icing. The roof halves don't match stylistically and the back of the house has been completely neglected – just like a real house in winter. When the house was being constructed, our gung-ho attitude was intercepted by the fact we were about to run out of the provided candy, so we turned to the Halloween candy in the cabinet, which was still abundant because my son trick-or-treated for three hours and there's enough sweets to feed an military base. Red and green hard candies make for festive décor, but the rainbow Skittles are the wrong shade and size and the Kit Kat bars jammed into a snow bank on the side make little to no sense stylistically.

The ramshackle icing house weighs more than a dozen bricks and when I toss it in the trash, it nearly puts a hole in the floor. It could probably withstand a nuclear bomb and won't begin to decay for another five Christmases.

The outdoor decorations come down easy. Going up, there was hours of cursing, but coming down, well, there was still cursing, but it was limited to about 15 minutes. Unlike the indoor decor that needs painstaking placement alongside other thin-glass trinkets, which are packed like eggs into their designated box slots, I grab the end of an outdoor light string and yank it off the house like Quasimodo's church bell rope. The lights crash down and staples ricochet around the porch like flies in a bouncy house. When the lights went up, there was meticulous measurements and math; the checking of lights and electricity. The equipment was laid out and organized like a surgeon's tools. Coming down, everything's helter-skelter. The lights that were carefully coiled from last year are crumpled like paper balls and tossed in the plastic storage container like a wastebasket. The red bows that donned our candy cane posts are carelessly mixed with green garland and electric cords, creating a seasonal salad that future me will be forced to untangle in 10 months.

Once everything has returned to normal... the plants are pushed into their rightful corners, the table legs are fitted into their proper carpet indents, and the picture frames are leaning on the end tables -- you realize how boring everything is. Hours before, there was cursing about Christmas décor deep into the new year. But now, the twinkling lights that turned your world into a magical wonder-land are boxed and gone. The light that currently illuminates the room comes from a fist-sized bulb that spotlights down upon your miserable existence like a prison tower. Nothing brightens the spirits more than hundreds of tiny white lights setting your world aglow. They sparkle and dance and make even the most mundane tasks more enjoyable. No one has ever gotten sentimental staring into the glow of a 60-watt soft white bulb.

But, you can rest assured knowing the glow of the sun will set your heart afire when it returns to the sky in just a few short months.

Holi-i-Day
Equal-i-Tay

America is a melting pot! You hear that term a lot, don't you? We're a melting pot! And for the most part it's true. And not because we melt cheese in a pot and dip our chips inside. Although we do that too. We're a melting pot because we have different cultures, religions and races from all over the world living in this great country of ours. It's what makes America… AMERICA!

But we're not necessarily a melting pot when it comes to our religious celebration breaks. The holiday calendar and the times in which our children get off from school, and adults off from work, is still centered around the Christian calendar. Christmas and the Christian holidays rule the timeframe in which we enjoy a long weekend. And I guess that's fine as long as everyone is cool with that. Is everyone cool with that?

I know over the last few years we've made more concessions in our work and school breaks for Jewish holidays. But I'm not sure we cut back in other areas. It seems like my son has about two months off at Christmas time and then again for Spring break and then Easter break and then some other kind of break, and then the whole summer off. Do kids go to school anymore? When I was in school, I went to school every day, 13 months a year for 27 years. Is it any wonder our country is 39th in education out of all the industrialized nations on Earth? Did I just pull that number out of my ass?

Yes!

But this isn't about our terrible education system. It's about how we divide our time between all the religions. Being the lazy agnostic/Catholic that I am, I have no clue as to when any of the Islamic holidays are and how long they would celebrate them for. I know Ramadan is a really long holiday and we can't take a month off to celebrate it, but can't we squeeze in a few days off for it? I think so. Considering a billion people celebrate it, it might be time to recognize it. As someone whose family is Catholic, I'm more than willing to give up Easter so that someone can have the time to do something. Don't the Hindus have a say in this?

Maybe it's time for all the religions to pick one holiday in which we ALL take some time off and we move on from there. Start staking some calendar tent poles. Why do we have so many calendars? Can't we have just one calendar? Is it really necessary to have so many different new years' celebrations? Can we agree to have just one? I know the Chinese have a great New Year. Maybe we can celebrate that one. I happen to like the color red, dragons, Chinese food and Chinese people, so maybe I'm biased. I'm not crazy about firecrackers though. Have you ever seen how much Chinese people can drink? They can drink like fish. I go to my local Chinese place and order take out and I leave shit-faced. They order tequila shots and refuse to let me go until I'm cross-eyed drunk. Damn fine people. Now I'm convinced we need to eliminate all New Years' celebrations and only do the Chinese New Year.

Most of us are just thankful to have some time off. Would you really care if you got a few days off for Ramadan? Of course not! I'd be totally psyched! If someone said, "hey, want a four day weekend?" I'd say, "Yes, please!" I may be a tad jaded here, but we're not jumping for joy because we have time off to worship, we're jumping for joy because we have a few days reprieve from our stupid bosses, lazy co-workers and generally monotonous work lives.

But there's only 365 days in the year and we do need to get some work done, so that's why we need to start staking some tent poles now. People don't like change, but we need to rework the holiday calendar a bit.

We'll keep Thanksgiving, of course. That's the warm-hearted American holiday when we killed off the Native Americans. So that's an automatic tent pole right there. I'm being sarcastic, of course—I truly love Thanksgiving and it's a day that is all about family and nothing more. It's also about food too. I love stuffing and whenever we eat it I say "Why don't we eat stuffing more often?" then I never do. It's like when I get a massage and say "Man, I'm going to get a massage every week" then three years goes by until

I get another massage.

Memorial Day is an essential holiday in giving a hearty thanks to our dead war vets. Labor Day is a particular favorite of mine as it's a day in which we do no labor at all. It should be called No Labor Day, but hey, it's time off from work no matter how you slice it. We have the all-important Fourth of July to celebrate the founding of our nation, but after that everything is up for grabs in my opinion. These three summer holidays involve a smoking grill and that's one of my favorite places to be besides a warm shower and bed. If I'm near a grill, I know I'll be eating something tasty, I'll be warm and most likely drinking a cool, fermented beverage.

Christmas is a HUGE tent pole. That will never change because our economy basically rotates around this cash-cow holiday. I love Christmas. My family loves Christmas because they get lots of good stuff. I don't want anything. I love Christmas because I really love... Christmas music. Weird, I know. Christmas music makes me delirious with joy, which you won't hear me say very often. I love all the 'I'll be by the fire' and 'Chestnuts on my nose' and all the other classics. There's about 8,922,367 different Christmas songs and I've heard them all. Give or take 33,412. I'll even listen to Christmas music in summer if it happens to hit the rotation on my iPhone.

Perhaps if holidays like Diwali and the Buddhist celebration of Vesak had a chance to be woven more into the fabric of our society, there'd be more songs about them.

Michael Bublé could release an album every month of chart-topping classics like "I'm Chipper for Yom Kippur" "Ramadan-a-ding-dong" and of course the Holi day classic "Colored powder gets in your eyes" as well as many other toe-tapping selections. Talk about an untapped market. I can smell the dollar signs already.

But we get big hunks of time off for the Christmas holiday and it's only fair that other religions get time off for their holidays too. Unfortunately, these holidays may not come at the most convenient times. If they're all crammed in at the same timeframe, we may have to close the country for two months while we drink and/or fast ourselves into a religious stupor. Someone may have to make some sacrifices and it may not be pretty. Some holidays are really not worth celebrating. Any Jew worth his salt will pretty much tell you that Hanukkah is a nothing holiday that got trumped up so their children had something to celebrate while their bratty friends got heaps of Christmas gifts. So maybe they agree for no time off for Hanukkah. I'm just throwing out ideas here—don't get upset.

Yom Kippur bounces around the calendar a bit, so perhaps the Jews take Yom Kippur as their big holiday, keep a consistent date and take a week off for that at the end of September. I know, I know. There's probably some kind of God frowning down upon me right now, but we must make sacrifices, right? Isn't that what Yom Kippur is all about? Sacrifices? …I think? ….Anyone?

So, let's have a review. Here's how I think things could work out if we keep an open mind. Let's have Yom Kippur around, let's say September 20th-ish, Navariti (Hindu festival of worship) around October 15th-ish, we can keep Thanksgiving where it is and then Christmas on December 25th. That's a good start! Then we celebrate the Chinese New Year and forget all these freakin' famous birthdays and bust our asses straight through till about April where we can celebrate Ramadan around April 15th-ish. And don't get me started on Scientology. That's a whole different subject in itself.

Once we get the big holidays locked up, we can work on the smaller ones. Trust me, no one in my family is going to cry if we don't have off for Easter, but I can tell you now that I'd really look forward to having a few days off in August, and then September, and then October, and then November and then end the year with big ol' chunk of Christmas/New Years break and start the new year off refreshed.

Maybe we can start making up some new holidays—not just celebrating the same old holidays. That seems very American and democratic. Maybe we can have a committee and see if we can get a round table discussion about coming up with a new holiday. How does God Day sound? Or maybe, Holy Worship Day? I don't know. I'm just throwing out ideas. As long as I have a three-day weekend, I don't really give a crap.

Microwaves and Diamond Rings

"We're getting rid of the microwave because we don't need it."

That's the announcement I get from my wife as I enter the kitchen on a clear afternoon on September 24. Not "Hello, dear, how was your day?" Not "You're the best!" I don't even have time to ask about her day... her *birth*day. I'm not expecting her to spin around and present me with a freshly baked apple pie... apron tied tightly around her waist. But I'm certainly not expecting this info bomb. Somewhere she heard microwaves are dangerous and now ours is dangerous. Our close friends don't have one! When someone mentions to them "I don't see a microwave in your kitchen," they act as if they're boxes made from weapons-grade plutonium. I've had a microwave for 35 plus years. I consider it an essential kitchen item. Indispensable even. It heats everything from gravy to popcorn in milliseconds.

But apparently, we're European now... two-hour lunches, siestas and closing up shop in the middle of the day to the detriment of businesses all over the area... that type of thing. Like the time I went to Paris and the entire city closed down for lunch and I couldn't find a pen. I spent two hours hunting for a pen to write something down and couldn't because the entire city was shuttered. Unfortunately, whatever thought I had to write down was lost forever and won't appear in this book.

In conclusion, reheating a bowl of rice in milliseconds will now give way to a metal pot to heat it on the stove, which requires gas for the burner, the pot will need to be washed with water and effort to do the job—soap water gets into the environment and pollutes our drinking water. What appears to be a better way of life is actually killing the environment and wasting more time than it appears. Anti-microwave sentiment is actually killing our environment. And even worse, it's robbing us of our precious time. It's not a decision to be taken lightly... it's our livelihood at stake. Sure, it takes a few minutes longer to heat things, but it quantifies as time passes... in years we'll have wasted countless hours heating rice when we could have been writing or creating art, or zipping through a season of *The Bachelor*. This is her idea and I'll stand by it... this is a woman who shops at Costco hungry. Food-Stuffs she would of thought was garbage six hours earlier is suddenly the world's greatest invention... "yogurt tubes! Amazing. Let's get this crate of 824 yogurt tubes."

Only hours before this dreadful announcement, I was at the jewelers. Two checks had cleared, one from my job and one from a freelance gig I'd done a few months prior, and I confidently transferred money from savings into checking and nervously pulled the trigger on the final ring payment... the last chunk of money on the expensive rock set in shiny platinum. To a caveman, completely worthless because it's inedible. To the modern man, some representation of wealth and prestige. A status symbol. To a modern woman, a cat's toy that flips the eyes into gleaming saucers. But to the practical man, a worthless tool when the zombie apocalypse spreads through his sleepy little town.

The jeweler asks me when I plan to give it to my wife and I tell him for our anniversary in November, which is a solid two months away, so he suggests I keep it in a safe place. "Not on the car seat" chimes his sister from the back. I joke that I plan to toss it in a paint can in my workshop and we chuckle way too hard over the absurdity. I assure him that I'm going to keep it in the large safe at my parent's house, which is a load of shit. I actually *do* stuff the ring into an old paint can and plunk it down on the workbench of my workshop amongst the other drippy paint cans. It's a perfect cover because the workshop is a dank cesspool. I don't want to tell my parents about the ring because they'll panic and tell me how expensive it is even though I just bought the thing and I know how expensive it is.

But my parents have always equated the value of life with how things cost, and not by what is actually valuable... time. In my life, in accordance with my parents, you simply don't talk about money. Let me rephrase that statement... they constantly talk about money; they don't talk about *spending* money. It's met with a sudden bombastic, hyperbolic sense of anxiety. My parents have been saving for retirement since the moment they opened a bank account and it's driven them mad with a scrambling sense of savings panic. It will *never* be enough and it's impossible to be comfortable, knowing that retirement will come.

Telling my parents you went out for a burger is to tell them you bought a vintage Porsche.

"Burgers? That's kind of expensive!"

Then it continues with eyebrow-raising inquiries as to *where* you got burgers...

"Really? Where'd you go?"

If you tell them, it may be met with severe disappointment, like when I failed sociology in college.

"Meehan's? That place is kind of expensive, yea?"

And then before you know it, you're justifying sirloin over ground chuck. So it's best not to tell them about the ring... or burgers... or anything. My wife and I have gotten to the point where we simply pretend we don't do anything.

"What'd you do this weekend?" they ask.

"Us? Stared at the wall..."

Of course, having a child who gives up the goods is problematic. Fortunately, he's exactly like I was as a kid... has the worst freakin' memory... can't remember what you told him five minutes ago. Although he'll drop a bomb on Christmas morning at my parent's house and spill an itemized list of everything I got my wife in descending price order.

I will give my parents credit though. At least they have a retirement plan. My retirement plan involves a car, and me driving over a cliff in a tragic accident for the life insurance money.

But the ring's been paid for and I have a level of comfort in the fact that the deed is done. It's difficult to drop many thousands of dollars on a shiny rock... it feels wrong, but it's what she wants and I'm willing to do it. The fingers need shiny rocks on them... that's just the way life works. We're sophisticated creatures. It's what separates us from animals. We shit in fresh water, have a box in our kitchen that keeps our dead meat cold, we prance around on spiky shoes and wear polished rocks on our arm sticks.

•••

My wife's September birthday is the beginning of the holiday crunch countdown. Time is flying by. In mid-January we'll be talking about how it was just Christmas and how fast the year is going.

"I'm still writing last year's date on my checks!"

Then the kids will be going back to school at the end of summer...

"The summer just flew by! I can't believe it."

Then we'll be talking about the holidays again...

"Christmas? Oh, God! Don't get me started! I can't

even! It was just Summer!!"

The eternal rush. Back-to-school ads at the beginning of Summer. Christmas in September. We never enjoy the moment. It's not possible. We celebrate Rita's birthday with takeout food on the beach... shrimp korma and chicken fingers. On the way, my son is already talking about Christmas, which is three months away. I clutch my purse strings. My money is already being spent and it gives me jitters. I can feel the ghost of Christmas future... it's called the January credit card bill. I just gave my wife a cheap greeting card filled with expensive cash for her birthday. My son drew balloons on a folded piece of copy paper. He got out of the deal easy. I've got jewelry to expense and their favorite holiday is breathing frosty air down the back of my neck. Max insists on eggs and bacon on Christmas morning. At least I can check something off the endless holiday list... the Christmas breakfast menu is set. A load off my mind.

Our ten-year anniversary drops the day before Thanksgiving. I pull the ring from the paint can and it shines like a crazy diamond. Because it is a diamond. Didn't get stolen. A paint can is better than a safe! Rita and I go out to dinner at Honu, a fancy restaurant where we are tucked cozily next to a fireplace, as I requested. We talk about everything that has led up to that moment... the tree, the wish, the hieroglyphics in the little notebook... the ups and downs... the health issues and our amazing son.

Ten years before, when I gave her a simple silver engagement ring over plates of hamburgers at Flea Market, a French Brasserie in the East Village of Manhattan, Rita couldn't have been more confused. We were living together and having a baby, so we were married in spirit already. So when I proposed, she thought I was giving her a random gift. We laugh about that now.

A decade later, I present her with a diamond in platinum. She loves it. Of course she does. It's a pretty big diamond! I've nearly gone broke paying for it. Rita grew up on beans and rice, which is good because we'll be eating a lot of it for the next few years.

We try and enjoy our anniversary, but in reality it's DECEMBER. The holidays are here. They've *been* here... which means Christmas. The other holidays have been obliterated. It starts the mili-second Halloween ends... *before* Halloween ends. Wander the aisles of your local everything-mart and the plastic jack-o-lanterns are on sale. 50% off. The holly is snaking in. It's snuck in. It's here! Fuck Thanksgiving! Thanksgiving is a zone you need to tolerate before the blinking lights go up. Two months of Ho Ho Ho and All I Want For Christmas Is You. Don't get me started on Hanukkah and Kwanza and the others. You know the deal... and my birthday is tossed in there somewhere too... lost in time. Don't get me wrong, I love Christmas. Lots of people do. But it starts at the end of summer. It's out of control. I see red bows and jewelry ads while my nose is still sunburned.

I see a picture on Facebook or some other social manipulator... an African girl. Standing in a garbage dump. Holding an IV attached to what I assume is her mother, who is lying on the ground, rail-thin, eyes shut. Mom is dying. God knows of what... AIDS, Ebola. She stares off into the distance. Her look says it all. "What am I going to do?" It almost seems like too much. I realize there's poor sanitation and people are dying. But why are they dying in the middle of a garbage dump? Can they move a few 100 yards out of the dump? Or is the entire country a dump? It's an image that stings. Manipulated for impact or not, I don't know. I don't know what I'm seeing anymore. My eyes see but my mind doubts and my heart is stuck in the middle.

The December holidays can be the most wonderful time of the year. Good food, good friends and tons of powerful drinks with heavy creams and warm spiced wines. The holidays can also be a source of sadness for some, but there's always a glimmer of hope for the unemployed, the sick and the downtrodden even at this time of year. They say that it's better to give than to receive, and that's true. But our giving muscles should be working at full-strength during the whole year and not just in the middle chunk of December. Sliding a few bucks out of your wallet to help the less fortunate seems like a stunning act of kindness, but it's more a selfish act to warm the cockles of your own heart rather than helping others. Try giving in May after you've gotten your tax return instead of getting that obnoxious 75" HD plasma television you've been eyeballing.

As a child at Christmas, I was spoiled rotten by my grandparents and all my parents' siblings. I received an absurd amount of gifts. You would have thought I'd grow up to be a spoiled adult who expected everything to be given to me, but now that I'm older I couldn't care less about receiving holiday gifts. In fact, I don't want anything at all. There's nothing that I want or really need -- and if I do need it, I can buy it on my own. I've actually become more of a minimalist and enjoy the freedom (both mentally and physically) of owning very little. I feel comforted to know that at any temperamental moment, I can throw it all by the wayside and go backpacking around the planet a few dozen times... if the desire should arise.

One of the great horrors of the holidays is receiving a gift that you don't want or like. Not only do you have to strain your acting chops pretending to like it, you get depressed later on because you realize someone actually paid hard-earned money on something that you'll toss in your closet and not see again until you do a spring cleaning or move. I'm all-in on the capitalist ideals of the USA, but wasting money on dopey items is heartbreaking no matter how you slice it. I'm not talking about so-called "bad" gifts like socks or even sweaters with doe-eyed kittens on them. Those tend to be useful once you reach a certain age. I'm talking about mind-benders like grandfather clocks made of cheese or a 50-inch turquoise felt sun-hat that Goldie Hawn sported in a magazine back in 1981. Even something as thoughtful as a man's wallet can be wince-inducing if it's red leather with giant white stitching. This is probably why the gift certificate is so popular these days. People realize taste is a personal thing and pink jumpsuits should be left to certain sections of our population, and not staring up from the lap of your nephew on Christmas morning... Unless he asked for a pink jumpsuit.

The absolute worst gifts to receive are those regifted. The dreadful holiday regift is doubly horrifying because it's blatantly obvious that the gift was shifted from one party to the next. It's embarrassing to receive because you were either forgotten about in the first place or given something no one wanted. It's possible the regift you receive has been regifted four or five times. If little Johnny gets a box of chocolate-covered prunes, you know something went terribly wrong down the chain. It gets to the point where people can't remember what's in the wrapping anymore and handing off a regift could be a game of Russian Roulette. "Oh look, you gave our six year-old a set of fireplace matches; something she's always wanted."

One year when I was 18, my parents' friends gifted me a box of pumpkin candy. I took it with a smile as I'm not one to turn down a free gift—I came to their house with nothing and left with something. But what was so ham-handed about this gift was it was in Thanksgiving-like packaging. Not only was it regifted, it was regifted from a different holiday. Halloween candy would have been preferential to Thanksgiving pumpkin candy. I like pumpkin, but from October 1st through the end of November, everything that's made into food is made with pumpkin and I feel candy is one thing that should be exempt. To add insult to injury, the pumpkin candy box looked as though it'd been stomped by a pack of wild boars. The cellophane wrapping was tearing in multiple spots and each box corner was at certain levels of crushed. At that point it should have been tossed in the garbage. Basically, I was the garbage man in this one-sided gift exchange. "We were going to toss this in the trash, but we gave it to you instead." Hey, you know the saying... I was once disappointed that I had no hat until I met a man with no head. Take what you get and make the best of it.

But sometimes no gift is just as good, and sometimes better, than a poorly decided regift. My friend Chip once got a wooden cane as a gift. He was a healthy and vigorous fifteen year-old, but his uncle thought a beat-up wooden cane would be something he would appreciate. Two days later, Chip whittled the thing into a lethal weapon that was used to stab a punching bag till it bled sand, so perhaps his uncle was correct. But it's best to err on the side of caution. When someone walks into your house, hand them a cookie or a stiff cocktail. They'll forget about gift exchanging in no time.

•••

It's the very beginning of January 2020, Just after a celebration I dislike... New Year's Eve. I don't really like going around telling everyone to have a Happy New Year until we've properly mourned the death of the old year. I've never felt particularly great when December 31st rolls around. I usually feel static and depressed—a bit muddy, I suppose. While most people have glitter-laden cardboard hats glued to their hair, prancing about in black-tie attire and sipping cheap champagne, I prefer to sit quietly at home and decompress.

The year worked very hard to give us the ups and downs that we enjoy reviewing at year's end. We make lists on the best of everything that happened during the course of the year—the best books, movies and television shows—these things will be neatly wrangled into a grouping and laid out for our light reading pleasure. Lists of restaurants, influential people, trends and whatever someone can conjure into a top-ten list. People like tight packages with things buttoned up for their ease of use and a top-ten list is pretty easy to swallow. Sometimes these lists start at the beginning of December, propelling us to exclaim, "Hey, there's 1/12th of the year left!" Especially since December is when filmmakers flood the market with their Oscar-bait releases. It seems premature to make a list of the year's events before December 31. But that's just me. Time magazine releases their person of the year in early December, but unless someone came along at the tail end and cured cancer, I guess that one was pretty much wrapped up.

My wife and I are standing in line at Zara, a giant clothing store, exchanging Christmas gifts she got a few weeks ago. There are 25 people on line. All have about five to seven articles of clothing. The process of checking out feels like an eternity. There are two cashiers. When a customer steps up, the cashier takes each article of clothing and scans it, shakes it, gently folds it, carefully places it down and punches what seems like 50 numbers into the monitor. The customer has coupons and a return... it fucking takes *forever*! I feel my life passing by... wasting away. It's painful. I'm a big fan of Apple computers. I think Steve Jobs was a genius. Total dick, but a genius. You can walk into an Apple store and buy a $12,000 computer in about three minutes and be out the door. Have these companies learned nothing from the Apple process? No need for lines. Check out is seamless and easy. It's the wave of the future. I'm on line at Zara for 25 minutes. It's ridiculous. You'd have thought they were giving away clothes, but this a line to actually *pay* for clothing. My wife hates my impatience, but I point out to her that my life is trickling away. You know what you can do in 25 minutes? Change the world! And it's not just these 25 minutes. It's all the 25 minutes of all the waiting lines combined. I can't be alone in this thought. We're given the gift of life, yet I am spending it staring blankly at the wall for 25 minutes, waiting to buy an overpriced shirt made by the small hands of slave children from a country we're currently bombing.

This is when I truly feel the weight of mortality. Death, in the end, will be one fell swoop. BAM! Over quickly... hopefully, if you're lucky, and not a long-suffering painful death like cancer or being crushed in half by a piano on the sidewalk. But death can also come in little chunk -- in small scoops from your soul -- in tiny doses throughout the day. Like smoking a cigarette or standing in line at Zara.

We get home from exchanging the gifts. It's been a degrading and tortuous affair. I flop onto the couch and flip on the a Knicks basketball game. After a tax commercial, I'm presented with a woman so elated, you'd have thought she'd been crowned queen of the Earth. She spins and faces us as her obnoxious husband wraps a *huge* diamond neck-lace around her outstretched neck. It's almost Valentine's Day. Time to show your love by spending your life savings on a strand of polished rocks. It takes all my energy to keep from throwing the remote through our 75" HD TV.

The
Mall

The mall is either the greatest invention in shopping, or the worst. I haven't decided yet.

Apparently this guy Victor Gruen invented the shopping mall, but I find that hard to believe, because the mall, an encapsulated, multi-shop hub is definitely the idea of a villainous hive-mind. There's no question it took a committee of criminals to create an idea as brilliantly stupid as the mall. But if Gruen truly was the mastermind of the mall, we have the Nazis to thank/blame for it. Gruen was an architect who escaped Nazi occupied Austria during World War II, came to America and invented the mall. Thanks/Fuck You, Nazis!

Like Gruen, the Nazis also enjoyed funneling large groups of people into one place, and look how that turned out!

For those of you living in a cave, or perhaps, in a civilized country where Capitalism isn't pounded into the culture like a pile-driver, the mall is a series of boxes that have various specialty items in them. Stores and shops. Not unlike those little cereal packs you get with eight different mini cereal boxes… like Frosted Flakes, Sugar Pops and Rice Krispies. My favorite being Apple Jacks because not only are Apple Jacks delicious, AJ is the acronym and that's always the right way to start the day – disregarding the fact that cereal has no nutritional value whatsoever. Whenever anyone took the box of Apple Jacks before I got to them, it would basically ruin my day, and sometimes my *week*. The remaining seven cereals were tolerated until we could get a fresh 8-pack.

Like this cereal example, the mall has a store for just about everyone. Sometimes two or three stores are to your liking, and sometimes, all of them have some appeal.

This is the love/hate relationship I have with the mall. I want to buzz around the mall and get what I need, but if I go to the mall with my wife, hours pass and I'm on my second meal of the day in the godforsaken place. The mall is loaded with places for her. I think scientists created some stores with women in mind… maybe some mathematicians too. Maybe Nazi mathematicians. They took the square root of clothing, multiplied it by the amount of accessories you can pair them with, divided it by the mental capacity of their loved ones to tolerate it all, and the sum is The Gap. Divide by 2 and you get Forever 21. Times it by two and you get Banana Republic. Times it by ten you get Bloomingdales, and time it by 100 you get Saks Fifth Avenue.

My wife Rita talks about the clothing she bought at

the mall years ago. Like it was a major milestone in our life.

"I'm wearing the jean jacket we bought at the Levi's store when we first met!"

I nod my head, but of course I don't remember. I don't walk down memory lane thinking about the clothing of the past. Sometimes she'll spring a mall pop quiz on me.

"Remember where we bought this bracelet?"

I tell her no because I only have limited capacity for recollection in my head and it's not being used on her wardrobe history. That memory chip is being used for important information: like wondering how Indiana Jones was able to ride on the outside of a Nazi submarine in *Raiders of the Lost Ark*. Maybe Victor Gruen could lend some insight into that.

If my wife and I walk by a men's store, she points and tells me I need new pants. I inform her the pants I'm wearing are fine... they're going on 8 years and still have no holes. She says I need *more* than one pair of pants, which is obviously absurd. Who needs more than one pair of pants? I'll buy new pants when the pair I'm wearing develops holes. The stores she patronizes, the pants already have holes in them. They're shredded like they've gone through the tiger cage at the Bronx Zoo. I go a decade and earn my holes. It's a badge of honor. Sometimes it can take 12, 15 years, but eventually I get those holes. People PAY for holes. It's ridiculous!

To compound the endless racks of clothes and deep aisles of trinkets, there's the terrible salespeople to contend with. Salespeople have been known to blatantly lie about something knowing you won't return it when you realize it's junk. A good chunk of selling is knowing people won't make the trip back because their time is more precious than getting back in the car, complaining, waiting in line, getting the money back, etc…

Like at the giant baby store in my mall. I have a kid and I've been through the whole baby thing, and there's no doubt you don't need half the baby stuff you think you do. Baby showers are wonderful occasions so you don't have to buy a lot of this crap, but walking through the giant baby store and zapping everything with those purchase guns is a slippery slope to go down.

Your baby is basically a blob of flesh for the first six months and does nothing but eat, sleep, poop and cry. So really, all you need is a crib, diapers & ointments, clothing, a carriage/stroller, bottles (or other things in that feeding area i.e. breast pump) and things like a thermometer and other health monitors. THAT'S IT! The people at the baby store make it seem like your kid will walk out of the house if you don't have every conceivable base covered before it's brought into the world. "Better get three or four different kinds of bottles and nipples. If your baby doesn't like one, he won't eat!" I challenge anyone to try and stop their child from eating when they're hungry. My son would have sucked the flesh off my finger if I'd stuck it in his mouth.

We have four malls in my immediate area and they

all have a Macy's. Those are the sadists who have that horrible Thanksgiving Day parade every year. They've designed the store like a maze, using glass cases filled with perfume and creams, so you can't escape once you're inside. It works! You rotate around the place and you see the Channel No. 5 station you've passed 6 times already.

It's like that movie Labyrinth. You go around and around and you see the same creatures over and over... like Muppets. Some even resemble David Bowie. They pop out and terrify you. I'm talking about the perfume women giving out free samples. They're frightening on multiple levels. First off, they're wearing enough make-up for a circus clown. Secondly, they're WAY too enthusiastic. Third, they've been standing in a cloud of perfume dust for weeks and it gives them this buzzing edge to their personalities— sort of a vapor psychosis.

You can walk by them eight times and they'll say the same thing over and over again, like they've never seen you before.

"Crimson Roses by Calvin Klein?"... "Crimson Roses by Calvin Klein?"

Like a motion sensor robot. After a while, you actually start to cave because you're having a mix of sympathy and some weird attraction to the scent, which is wafting off them like steam. The thing is, for men, this is kryptonite. But if a woman gets a spritz on her wrist, she'll hold it to your nose and say "Isn't this nice?" Which is code for: "Wouldn't you like to buy this for me?" Those perfume robot women are sneaky good.

Sometimes I'll enter a store and the salesperson is right on top of me asking if I need help and I'm like "NO! Leave me alone." But, ten seconds later when I can't find the thing I want, I turn for help and of course, they've disappeared. They go in the back and take a coffee break that lasts 15 hours.

"She was just freaking here a minute ago" I mutter to myself. Then I ask the new guy... it's obvious he's new because he's 16 and he's growing a bad moustache... so I ask him and he looks around for the girl who just went on a 15-hour coffee break. Probably in Colombia. After he disappears I just leave the store. He'll be gone for 23 hours.

My mall also has a vitamin store and the people who work there have the enthusiasm of a personal trainer. They shout everything at steroid levels and run around the store as an example of a healthy person who's jacked to the gills on vitamins.

"Be super energetic. LIKE ME!"

I used to work in a vitamin store and it was our Prime Directive to HOUND customers. We wanted them to buy two of everything and the most expensive choice if possible. Apparently, all the vitamin shops use this tactic and still do as I'm always hounded by the salesperson in the vitamin shop. Even if I'm just browsing, they'll ask me four times if I need help. And if I DO need help—oh Boy! They act as if I'll DIE if I don't buy what they're selling because they're supplying me actual LIFE!

Most people don't know anything about vitamins. If you go in needing calcium supplements, the salesperson will tell you five other things you need to help the calcium penetrate your blood with the highest impact or you're simply throwing your money down the toilet. If you don't buy it, they'll smile and give you a passive aggressive, "OK, no problem" but they shrug as if to say: "I don't give a shit, go ahead and DIE for all I care!" So if you're going in for a $5 bottle of multi-vitamins, be prepared to drop $100 on stuff that will sit in your kitchen cabinet for three years.

A lot of malls have mall walkers – people who are zipping around like little choo choo trains. They're quick-stepping around the place. You see a pack of 65 year-old ladies chugging towards you as you enter through the sliding doors and you think "Why are these three ladies going outside with no winter jackets on?" But nope, they hang a hard left – like a flock of birds, and chug back into the mall. They've got spandex and comfortable sneakers that didn't cost more than $45 at the shoe warehouse.

Teenagers go to the mall and hang out. They can't go to bars and drink yet, and sometimes the world outside is dark and dangerous - so they go to the mall. Mall security doesn't care. These are future shoppers. Pretty soon they'll have mindless jobs… maybe even jobs at the mall… and eventually spend their hard-earned cash on things like purses and oversized sweatshirts. They'll spend that money at the mall. The mall is like a breeding ground for consumerism. There's a Starbucks and a chocolate shop in the vicinity. Feel yourself losing a step and you can load up on caffeine and empty sugar calories and propel yourself into another bout of wallet-draining shopping.

Many malls have little booth kiosks. Those are the places that sell stuff even more worthless than the stuff in the stores. They can't afford rent with the crap they're hawking, so they have a tiny box in the middle of the throughway. It's unforgiving these kiosks. There's no bathroom or hideaway place. If you need to pick your nose, you must dig in plain sight.

A lot of these kiosks are jewelry booths. There's one right across from a high-quality chain jewelry store at my mall. I don't think the chain store was happy to see this kiosk suddenly "pop up." Shoppers prefer these little kiosks because the person running it is 19 years-old. There's no pressure. The people at the big jewelry store have the tendency to carefully undermine your taste if you start skimping on the price, and NO ONE likes to have their taste questioned—not even the guy wearing a pink tank-top, black & white checkered pajama bottoms with brown leather cowboy boots. If you're not careful, the best jewelry salesperson can manipulate you into a high-end purchase, just to spite them! The jewelry salespeople have a stone-cold smile/scowl, with eyes squinted just enough to shield you from their vision, as you probably disgust them. They can be flippant and have an air of superiority, so to avoid being around them, avoid jewelry shopping just to browse. Jewelry shopping is something to take seriously and not to kill time. If you want to kill time, go to the electronics store and watch the basketball game on 30 HDTVs simultaneously.

The mattress store at my mall used to be a big kiosk, but they graduated to an actual space. Business was booming. The customers walk in now and see nothing but giant white boxes lying around. Most people go into a mattress store with a budget of $400 and realize they have two mattresses available in the showroom in that price range— and those are one-hour motel quality. Within seconds, they have to think outside the box spring. The salespeople like to hang over you, creepily, while you're lying on the mattress testing it out.

"Comfortable, huh?" They say nodding like a pimp.

They don't have to do much to sell their product. They say:

"Well, you spend half your life on a mattress, so you might as well get the best."

Actually, you spend about 1/3 of your life on a mattress, but they're right. Spine alignment is nothing to skimp on. By the time you're finished, you've dropped two grand on the mattress, box spring, delivery and all the other stuff you forgot to calculate when you walked in the door. Better enjoy the mattress because the only thing you'll be able to afford to do is sleep for the next few months. And if you do more than sleep, be prepared to reference the baby section mentioned in previous paragraphs.

My fancy mall also has stores on the outside of the mall. Perhaps this is a space issue. They wanted to get a store *inside* the mall, but had to settle for *outside* the mall. It's ATTACHED to the mall, but not in the carefree strolling area. You have to go outside and that sort of defeats the purpose of the hub system. Perhaps the rents are cheaper.

"The pillow store is outside? I guess we're not going there."

The pillow store's impulse buying customer is seriously reduced. No one travels outside for pillows. If pillows are being offered in the warm comfort of the mall's enclosure where music is playing and the smell of coffee is in the air… maybe.

Every mall has a store that makes you wonder how it stays in business. The bathing suit store doesn't flourish in the winter and I'm pretty sure the 8 tee-shirt shops are cancelling each other out. My mall had a Bonsai tree store, which was really cool. For years I gave Bonsai trees as Christmas gifts, but as soon as the Bonsai tree store opened in the mall, I never gave one as a gift again. I saturated my own market. The one person I never bought a tree for was myself and the day I went to buy one, the Bonsai store went belly up.

Christmas at the mall is another kind of Hell. If there's one thing that can drive you to an early grave, it's the whole 'Sitting on Santa's lap' situation. It doesn't matter if you're a parent, photographer, person-wrangler or even a kid – it's a massive, twisted ball of stress. Crying, urinating, yelling – and that's the parents! The kids are even worse! Walk by the crush of humans waiting for Santa and the second-hand anxiety is palpable.

I watch as a young couple is scooping their three kids, all under the age of five into Santa's Den of Iniquity and I need a stiff cocktail. The father is aging by the minute. You can see his odometer spinning and his hair graying before our eyes. Mom is in a $500 sweater and looking fabulous – somehow, keeping it all together, but for the grace of God, she's going to get this motherfucking photo taken and have it on the mantle – or else! The kids have no clue what's going on and are trying to make a prison break. They're working together. One goes left the other goes right. It's a nightmare. I thank the universe my kid is 13. He aged out of the madness. Now the only time I'll visit the mall Santa is when I'm drunk and want to get a photo with my drunken friends.

Being a mall Santa is actually a pretty cushy job. They're well paid. These men are being paid not only to sit and take pictures with babies, but reaping the benefits of sitting on their fat asses at home all year long, drinking beer and never shaving their faces. They're elderly and becoming morbidly obese has finally benefitted them. I'm planning on this kind of semi-retirement job in the future if my heart doesn't rupture from all the fatty foods I'm swallowing.

The people who work at the Santa photo table are machines. They're punching people through like human cattle. "Come here – go – turn – sit – tell Santa what you want – come this way – what package do you want? – press this button – that's $185." The photo package people are sneaky pushy salespeople. They'll convince you that you need a Santa photo for every member of your family. For some reason, they have photo packages with 18 wallet-sized photos. Nobody carries wallet photos anymore! Who are these people? They also have the photo package that seems expensive for the three photos they're giving you, but for $5 more, they'll give you 25 more photos… all of which will sit in a drawer and never see the light of day. The extra photos seem like a good deal when you're on line and the family of seven kids behind you are screaming down your neck, but once you get home, you realize there aren't enough members in your family to give these photos to.

Christmastime is actually my favorite time of the year at the mall because I go alone. My wife wants to come, but I make it clear that this is a solo run… a one-man job. I'm buying her gifts. She's not allowed to see them. That's not how Christmas gift-giving works! At the mall I take one long, twisty stroll through the place, buy all the stuff I need, and then I'm out. I'll eat ONE meal, probably drink a beer… maybe two… not more than three or I buy dumb shit. Then I'm done. If I drink too much and shop, I make questionable decisions.

"I don't know, I thought a brass urn was kind of

cool for you."

The rest of the shopping will be done online. Shopping online is fun because when a package comes to my door it's like a little Christmas gift. Even if it's not for me.

"Oohh! Trash bags! Just what I wanted!"

I'm not sure Gruen saw the future potential of the mall when he made blueprint copies of his first mall layout: the mall Santas, the kiosks… the expensive car parked in the middle of the foyer that no one can afford. Did he envision packs of roaming teens yelling and drinking coffee? Did he know about food courts and the potential to get any kind of fast food you wanted in a room filled with mouth-breathing lunatics sitting on cheap metal chairs? Did he know that fellow architects would design and build structures calculated to get humans lost and double-back over and over so as to never leave the place? Did he have a vision of broken escalators, water fountains, limited benches to sit on, and 30 different clothing stores all in a row?

We don't have the answers. Perhaps he just wanted a place to shop so he didn't have to drive all over town to get what he needed. That place didn't exist, so he created it… with the other 20 evil humans that he worked with (some of them potentially Nazis). Gruen laid the foundation for not only the mall, but for the ultimate shopping structure that would become part of the human experience.

God help us all.

Holiday terms you couldn't possibly know unless you looked them up or lived 175 years ago.

Tidings = News

Sugarplum = Hard candy made with fruit

Figgy pudding = Steamed fruitcake with booze

Hark = Listen!

Yule = Germanic winter festival

Frankincense = Aromatic resin from a Boswellia tree

Mrryh = Aromatic resin from a Commiphora tree

Troll = Sing loud

Bobtail = Short horse tail

Auld lang syne = Times long past.

King Wenceslas = Wenceslas I was a Prince (not a king apparently) of Bohemia from 921 to 935

If you, or someone you know is contemplating suicide, please call or text the Suicide Hotline at 988. They are also available online at: <u>988lifeline.org</u>.

These services are completely free, confidential and available 24 hours a day, seven days a week.